the
ASPARAGUS FESTIVAL
Cookbook

REVISED

by Jan Moore, Barbara Hafley,
Glenda Hushaw & Jacqueline Zupo

CELESTIAL ARTS
Berkeley

Celestial Arts and the Celestial Arts colophon are registered
trademarks of Random House, Inc.

Library of Congress Cataloging-in-Publication Data
available from the publisher

ISBN-13: 978-1-58761-174-2

Cover design by Chloe Rawlins
Text design by Brad Greene
Cover photo by Belcher Photography

First Edition

146086900

Table of CONTENTS

☞ Measuring Asparagus

APPROXIMATE NUMBER OF SPEARS
IN 1 POUND OF ASPARAGUS

Colossal Size	7 or fewer stalks not < 1" in diameter
Jumbo	7-10 stalks not < $13/16$" in diameter
Large	11-20 stalks not < $7/16$" in diameter
Standard	21-30 stalks not < $5/16$" in diameter
Small	31-45 stalks not < $3/16$" in diameter

Diameter is measured at the point 9 inches down from tip

FRESH ASPARAGUS YIELDS

1 pound, trimmed	2 cups, cut up
1 pound, trimmed	four $1/2$ cup servings, cooked
1-1$1/2$ pounds	1 pint, frozen
2$1/2$-4 pounds	1 quart, canned
2 cups, chopped	1 cup purée

PROCESSED ASPARAGUS YIELDS

1 quart, frozen	2 cups, grated
1 10-ounce package	1$1/4$ cups, cut up
1 14-ounce can	1$1/3$ cups, cut up

A Few Words of Praise

If ever a vegetable deserved a cult following, it is asparagus! Poets have sung the praise of asparagus; artists have painted it; craftsmen have recreated it; photographers have captured it; healers have prescribed it; epicures have sighed over it; and kings have been inspired by it!

When the city of Stockton, California, decided to launch a festival to support community projects, charitable groups, and service organizations, asparagus—the "Rolls Royce of the Vegetables"—was the most likely choice as Stockton sits in the heart of asparagus country. Stockton hosted its first Asparagus Festival in 1986 at the beautiful Oak Grove Regional Park. The three-day event, always held on the fourth weekend in April, attracts some 100,000 asparagus lovers and soon-to-be converts.

Highlighting the Festival is the big-top tent dubbed "Asparagus Alley" where gourmet asparagus dishes are prepared to delight Festival goers. Featured in this cookbook are favorites like

5

Deep-Fried Asparagus (literally tons of asparagus are used), Asparagus Bisque (sheer ambrosia), and Asparagus Pasta (perfect for pasta lovers).

What other vegetable is as much a delight to eat as it is healthy for you? Asparagus contains significant amounts of vitamins C and B_6, thiamine and potassium, has more folacin per serving than any other vegetable, and is high in fiber and low in salt too! All the recipes here are guaranteed to please your palate and help you on your way to good health. Cook, eat, and savor the wonderful way of asparagus!

APPETIZERS:
Stalking the Asparagus

All recipes require cleaned and trimmed asparagus.

Stockton Aparagus Festival
DEEP-FRIED ASPARAGUS

1/2 cup cornstarch

3/4 cup flour

1 tsp. each salt and baking powder

1/4 tsp. black pepper

1/2 tsp. each white pepper, celery salt,
   and baking soda

2 egg whites

2/3 cup cold, flat beer

3 lbs. asparagus, trimmed to 8-inch lengths

peanut oil

☞ Mix all ingredients except asparagus and oil in a bowl with a wire whisk until well blended. Dip asparagus individually in the batter and deep-fry them in at least 2 inches of peanut oil for 2 minutes or until golden brown.

Serves 6

ASPARADILLAS

8 oz. cream cheese, softened

$1/4$ cup mayonnaise

1 Tbsp. prepared mustard

10 fajita-sized flour tortillas

2 Tbsp. toasted sesame seeds

20 thin slices of deli-sliced ham

30 thin asparagus spears, blanched and cooled

10 thin strips each red bell pepper and
yellow bell pepper

☞ Combine cream cheese, mayonnaise, and mustard in a small bowl. Divide mixture evenly between the tortillas, then spread to cover. Sprinkle $1/2$ teaspoon sesame seeds on each tortilla and cover with 2 ham slices. Place 1 asparagus spear on the edge of the tortilla and begin to roll tightly, adding a red and yellow pepper strip and 2 more asparagus spears as you go. Roll the tortilla completely and fasten with toothpicks. Finish all the tortillas in same manner. Cut tortillas into 1-inch pieces to look like pinwheels. Discard ends.

Yield: 50 appetizers

9

Best Ever
ASPARAGUS DIP

> ³/4 cup well-cooked, drained, and mashed fresh
>   asparagus
> 4 chopped green onions, including tops
> 5 cooked and crumbled slices bacon
> 1 tsp. dill weed
> 1 pkg. ranch dip mix
> 1 cup each mayonnaise and sour cream

☞ Combine all ingredients, mixing well. Chill. Garnishing with asparagus tips is optional. Serve on crackers or as a vegetable dip.

Yield: Approximately 3 cups

Asparagus
SPEARS ELEGANTÉ

3 oz. cream cheese, softened

Prepared pesto to taste

8 slices prosciutto or thin ham

8 thin slices provolone cheese

8 6-inch asparagus spears, cooked to tender-crisp

☞ Combine cream cheese with pesto. Spread half of cream cheese mixture on prosciutto slices. Set aside.

Spread remaining cream cheese mixture on provolone cheese slices. Place 1 asparagus spear on one edge of cheese, then roll in jellyroll fashion. Place the roll on a prosciutto slice, wrapping the roll with the prosciutto in a spiral fashion. Refrigerate.

Yield: 8 appetizers

Asparagus `a la REBECCA

9 green onions, including tops
8 cups diagonally sliced fresh asparagus
Vegetable oil for frying
2 cups fresh parsley florets
5 large eggs
3/4 cups each Italian-style bread crumbs
   and grated Parmesan cheese
Salt to taste

☞ Slice green onions lengthwise into quarters; then into 1-inch pieces. Place in large bowl. Sauté asparagus in oil until limp (use oil sparingly). Add asparagus to onions, then add parsley and eggs. Mix well. Add bread crumbs, cheese, and salt. Mix well.

Heat oil in frying pan until quite hot. Shape 1 heaping tablespoon of asparagus mixture with your fingers while on the spoon so asparagus and onions mostly lie in same direction. Place in hot pan, keeping individual patties separate. Fry until brown, then carefully turn to fry other side. After turning, press down to flatten. When done, drain patties on paper towels.

Serve patties hot, room temperature, or cold. Can be served as a side dish or as an appetizer. Wonderful on top of thinly sliced French bread.

Yield: Approximately 48 3-3½-inch patties

Kelly Brothers and Sarah Gardner's ASPARAGUS ROLL-UPS

14 thin slices Peppridge Farm white bread,
    crusts trimmed
8 slices bacon, cooked crisp, crumbled
8 oz. cream cheese, room temperature
Finely grated zest of 1 lemon
28 asparagus spears, cooked crisp-tender
Melted unsalted butter

☞ Flatten bread slices by rolling over them with a rolling pin. Combine bacon, cream cheese and lemon zest. Spread an even layer of the cream cheese mixture on each flattened bread slice.

Place 2 asparagus spears, with tips facing in opposite directions, on each edge of each bread slice. Roll up each slice jellyroll fashion. Cut each roll in half and place seam down on a lightly greased cookie sheet.

Preheat broiler. Brush tops and sides of the roll-ups with melted butter. Broil 6 inches from heat until lightly browned and toasted. Serve immediately.

Yeild: 28 roll-ups

15

SPEAR-IT STICKS

8 5-inch asparagus tips, raw or lightly steamed
8 oz. cream cheese, softened
1 cup chopped walnuts

☞ Thoroughly dry asparagus. Coat each spear with cream cheese. Roll in walnuts. Refrigerate.

Serve cold.

Yield: 8 appetizers

Asparagus
TIDBITS

3 oz. cream cheese, softened
Prepared horseradish to taste
8 thin slices ham, smoked turkey, or dried beef
8 cooked asparagus spears, trimmed to fit meat

☞ Combine cream cheese with horseradish. Evenly divide mixture among meat slices, spreading on lower third of each slice. Place asparagus spear on top of the mixture at the edge of the slice; roll in jellyroll fashion. Chill until quite firm. Cut into bite-sized pieces, securing each with a toothpick. Arrange on a platter, garnish, and serve.

Yield: 24 pieces

ASPARAZINGERS

4 medium eggs
1 cup low-fat cottage cheese
1/4 cup flour
1 tsp. baking powder
2 Tbsp. canola oil
1/2 lb. bacon, cooked crisp then crumbled
3/4 cup cooked asparagus, cut into 1/4-inch pieces
2 oz. chopped green chilies
1 cup grated Monterey Jack cheese
Salt and white pepper to taste

☞ Preheat oven to 350°F.

Spray miniature muffin pans with nonstick spray; set aside. In food processor, blend eggs briefly and add cottage cheese. Pulse to blend. Add flour, baking powder, and oil; blend. Stir in bacon, asparagus, chilies, and cheese. Add salt and pepper. Spoon mixture into muffin pans. Bake for 20 minutes. Let cool slightly before serving.

To serve, place zingers on a bed of finely shredded red cabbage or finely shredded lettuce.

Yield: 18-24

Asparagus
JALAPEÑO DIP

16 oz. cream cheese, softened
8 oz. shredded jack cheese
1 Tbsp. each minced garlic and fresh chopped dill
1/4 cup chopped Jalapeño peppers
2 cups chopped asparagus
2 tsp. salt, or to taste

Mix all ingredients together. Chill. Serve with crackers or chips.

Yield: Approximately 3 1/2 cups

Delicious Delta Delights in CROUSTADES

CROUSTADES
1 1/2 loaves sourdough bread
1 cup butter or olive oil
Garlic cloves, peeled and mashed, to taste

FILLING
3 Tbsp. butter
2 Tbsp. minced parsley
1 Tbsp. each minced shallots and minced fresh basil
1 lb. asparagus, minced and blanched
1/4 cup minced fresh mushrooms
1 Tbsp. flour
1/4 cup Madeira wine
1 cup heavy cream
Grated Gruyere cheese to taste
Salt, white pepper, lemon juice, dried thyme,
    and nutmeg to taste

☞ Preheat oven to 375°F.

CROUSTADES: Slice the bread, then cut into 2-2½-inch rounds using a cookie cutter or wine glass. Melt butter or olive oil in a small skillet with the mashed garlic until garlic gives off aroma. Roll out the bread rounds with a rolling pin. Brush the bread and the cups of a mini-muffin tin with the mixture, then press bread into the cups. Bake for 10-15 minutes.

FILLING: Melt the butter in a skillet. Add parsley, shallots, basil, asparagus, and mushrooms. Sauté for 2 minutes. Add flour and stir for 2 more minutes. Add the wine and cream, then simmer until the sauce is thickened. Add the cheese, salt, white pepper, lemon juice, thyme, and nutmeg. Fill the croustades. Place croustades on a cookie sheet and broil until cheese melts.

Yield: Approximately 60 croustades

Dierdre Fitzpatrick's
FRENCH BREADED
ASPARAGUS

1 lb. fresh asparagus, cooked
1 egg
1 Tbsp. cold water
1/2 cup fine bread crumbs, dried
1 tsp. salt
1/4 cup Parmesan cheese
1 tsp. paprika
Vegetable oil for frying

☞ Beat egg and mix with cold water. Mix crumbs, salt, cheese, and paprika together. Dip asparagus in egg mixture then in crumb mixture. Chill 1 hour. Fry in hot oil until golden brown.

Yield: Depends on spear size of asparagus

22

Asparagus SEAFOOD ALMOND SPREAD

1 lb. fresh asparagus, cooked and finely chopped
12 oz. cream cheese, softened
1^1/2 cups ground almonds
^{3}/4 lb. fresh crab or shrimp meat
^{3}/4 cup mayonnaise
6 Tbsp. white wine or sherry
2 cloves garlic, pressed
2 tsp. prepared mustard
Finely chopped onion, to taste
Salt and pepper to taste

☞ Combine all ingredients together and mix well. Refrigerate mixture for several hours to allow flavors to blend.

Spread mixture on baguettes or crackers as a cold hors d'oeuvre or heat through to serve as a warm dip with crackers.

Yield: Approximately 6 cups

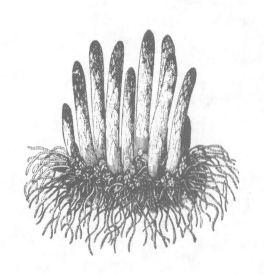

SALAD AND SOUP:
'Gras Clippings and Sippings

All recipes require cleaned and trimmed asparagus.

California
ASPARAGUS SALAD

1/4 cup olive oil

1/2 cup seasoned rice vinegar

Juice of 1/2 lime

1/2 tsp. ground cumin

1/4 tsp. each oregano, black pepper, and salt

1 1/4 lbs. fresh asparagus

3 boned, skinned, and cooked chicken breasts,
   cut into bite-sized chunks (other firm white meat
   may be substituted)

3/4 cup mayonnaise

1/2 tsp. curry powder

6-8 large tomatoes

Lettuce for garnish

☞ Combine oil, vinegar, and lime juice. Add cumin, oregano, black pepper, and salt. Blend well; set aside.

Reserve 2-3 inches of asparagus tips, then slice the rest diagonally into ¹/₂-inch pieces. Cook until tender but crisp; rinse with ice water; drain well.

Combine sliced asparagus, chicken, and oil mixture to coat evenly; marinate for 8-10 hours in refrigerator.

Combine mayonnaise and curry powder; mix well and refrigerate.

When ready to serve, core tomatoes making an 8-point star by cutting from the top of tomato almost to the bottom, but not completely through. Open tomato into a flower (smaller tomatoes may be scooped out to form a bowl).

Line individual serving plates with lettuce leaves. Place tomato on lettuce, then fill each tomato with asparagus mixture. Top with curried mayonnaise. Garnish mayonnaise with reserved asparagus tips.

Serves 6-8

27

Jackie's 'GRAS with CLASS

DRESSING
1 lemon
2 Tbsp. white vinegar
1/3 cup sugar
1 Tbsp. vegetable oil
2 tsp. poppy seeds

SALAD
1/4 cup sliced almonds
1 pkg. baby spinach
8 oz. raw or lightly steamed asparagus, thinly sliced*
1/2 medium cucumber cut in half, seeds removed and
    thinly sliced
1/4 small red onion, thinly sliced

☞ Zest lemon to yield $1/2$ teaspoon zest. Juice lemon to extract 2 tablespoons juice. Combine zest, juice, vinegar, sugar, oil, and poppy seeds in a small bowl. Whisk until well blended. Refrigerate.

Preheat oven to 350°F. Spread almonds in a single layer over the bottom of a baking pan. Bake 10-12 minutes or until lightly toasted. Cool almonds in pan.

Place spinach, asparagus, cucumber, and onion in a large serving bowl. Whisk dressing and pour over salad. Mix well. Top with almonds and serve immediately.

Serves 8 as a dinner salad or 4 as an entrée.

*Variations: fresh strawberries, apples, pears, oranges or a combination may be used.

ASPARAGUS
and CITRUS SALAD

2 Tbsp. finely chopped shallots

1 Tbsp. balsamic vinegar

1-2 Tbsp. sherry vinegar or dry sherry

4 oranges, preferably blood oranges

1-2 Tbsp. extra virgin olive oil

1/4 tsp. salt

Freshly ground pepper to taste

1 1/2 lb. fresh asparagus cut into 2-inch pieces
   and cooked to tender-crisp

4 Tbsp. coarsely chopped, toasted walnuts

☞ Combine shallots with vinegar and sherry in a small bowl. Let stand 20 minutes or more.

Zest 1 of the oranges. Avoid the white pith. Finely chop zest and add to the shallots. Squeeze $1/3$ cup juice from zested orange and add to the bowl. Slowly whisk in the olive oil and season with salt and pepper. Set aside.

Toss cooled asparagus with shallot mixture.

Remove ends of remaining oranges and peel, cutting down the fruit vertically. Slice horizontally into $1/2$-inch-thick slices. Arrange the orange slices and asparagus spears on salad plates and season to taste with additional salt and pepper. Top each serving with 1 tablespoon walnuts.

Serves 4

Fresh Asparagus
COUSCOUS SALAD

DRESSING

1 clove garlic, very finely chopped

6 scallions, white parts only, finely chopped
(reserve greens for salad)

6 Tbsp. lime juice

1 tsp. salt

Freshly ground black pepper

1/4 cup vegetable oil

3 Tbsp. chopped fresh dill

SALAD

1 cup finely chopped onion

2 Tbsp. vegetable oil

2 cups each fish or chicken stock, water, and couscous

3 lbs. asparagus, sliced diagonally into 1/3-inch slices;
reserve tips

1 1/3 cups radishes cut in half from top to bottom, then
cut into 1/4-inch slices reserved green scallion tops,
thinly sliced diagonally

1 lb. cooked small shrimp

32

☞ In a small bowl mix the garlic, scallions, lime juice, salt, and pepper. Set aside.

In a medium saucepan sauté the onions in oil over medium heat for about 4 minutes. Add the stock and water. Bring to a boil, then stir in the couscous, remove from heat, and cover. After 5 minutes, fluff with a fork and allow to stand 5 more minutes, then fluff again. Transfer to a large dish and refrigerate. As other ingredients are readied, remove and fluff every 10 minutes.

Blanch the asparagus until tender but crisp. Place into iced water for 2 minutes, drain and set on towels to absorb extra moisture.

Whip the oil into dressing with a fork, then stir in the dill. Mix the asparagus, radishes, green onions, shrimp, and dressing into the couscous. Serve over a lettuce leaf base, garnishing with the asparagus tips.

Serves 8

Ethan Harp's
ASPARAGUS TOMATO SALAD

DRESSING
2 Tbsp. lemon juice
1 Tbsp. olive oil
1 tsp. red wine vinegar
1/2 clove garlic, minced
1/2 tsp. Dijon mustard
1/4 Tsp. each dried basil and salt
1/8 tsp. pepper

SALAD
12 asparagus spears, cut into 1 1/2-inch pieces
3 small tomatoes, seeded and diced
1 small red onion, thinly sliced
Toasted sesame seeds (optional)

☞ Combine dressing ingredients; set aside. Cook asparagus in salted water until crisp but tender. Drain and cool. Combine asparagus, tomato, and onion; toss with dressing. Sprinkle with sesame seeds. Serve immediately.

Serves 2-4

Crispy
ASPARAGUS SALAD

DRESSING
1/4 cup white wine vinegar
2 Tbsp. chopped fresh basil or 2 tsp. dried basil
1 Tbsp. each vegetable oil and Dijon-style mustard
1 clove garlic, minced
1/2 tsp. salt
1/4 tsp. bottled hot pepper sauce

SALAD
3 cups thinly, diagonally sliced asparagus
1 cup each julienned jicama and sweet red pepper
2 Tbsp. minced onion
Broiled chicken or fish (optional)

Combine dressing ingredients and mix well.

Toss salad ingredients together and combine with dressing. Mix well.

*Serves 4 as dinner salad or 2 as main dish
with meat added*

Light and Fresh
ASPARAGUS SOUP

6 cups chicken stock

2 cups scallions, sliced diagonally (reserve 1/2 cup green tops)

1 1/2 lbs. asparagus, sliced into 1/4-inch rounds; reserve tips

3 Tbsp. lemon juice

1/3 cup cream or sour cream

1 1/2 tsp. finely chopped fresh mint

Pinch of cayenne pepper

☞ Bring chicken stock to a boil in a medium-large sauce pan; add 1 1/2 cups scallions and cook 10 minutes. Add the sliced asparagus stalks. Bring the soup back to a boil and simmer 5 minutes, then remove from heat.

While the soup simmers, bring 1 cup water to boil in a small saucepan. Cook the asparagus tips for 3 minutes; drain and refresh in cold water. Slice tips thinly; set aside.

Purée chicken stock mixture in small batches using a blender or food processor. Return to the saucepan and reheat. Add the lemon juice, cream, mint, pepper, asparagus tips, and reserved scallion tops. Lower the heat and stir well—do not boil.

Serve hot or cold. Soup may be garnished with equal parts yogurt and sour cream, or topped with an asparagus tip.

Serves 8

Stockton Asparagus Festival BISQUE

1/2 cup butter

3/4 cup flour

2 quarts whole milk

1 cup chicken stock (made from bouillon cube)

1 bay leaf

1 tsp. each white pepper and salt

3 cups cooked asparagus, cut into 1/2-inch pieces

Instant potatoes (use to thicken bisque if needed)

☞ In a stockpot, melt butter; add flour, stirring constantly so mixture doesn't burn. Add 1 quart milk slowly to roux, stirring constantly. When combined and thickened, add remaining milk and chicken stock. Add bay leaf, pepper, salt, and asparagus and cook slowly for 1 hour.

To serve, top bisque with large sourdough croutons and a spoonful of sour cream.

Yield: 1 gallon

Jan's Favorite
ASPARAGUS SOUP

3 chopped onions*
1/2 cup butter or margarine*
1 gallon water*
4 beef bouillon cubes (or more to taste)*
1-2 lbs. asparagus, sliced diagonally into
   1/8-inch pieces
Grated jack or Parmesan cheese to garnish

☞ Sauté onions in butter until they just begin to brown. Add water and bouillon cubes. Bring to a boil; add asparagus and cook about 3 minutes until barely tender. Serve with or without garnish.

*May substitute onion soup mix for these ingredients
Serves 6-8

ENTRÉES:
Asparagus Front and Center

All recipes require cleaned and trimmed asparagus.

Stockton Asparagus Festival PASTA

1 cup sliced fresh mushrooms

$1/2$ cup chopped green onions

4 cloves garlic, minced

$1/3$ cup olive oil

$1/2$ cup olive wedges

1 cup diced fresh or canned tomatoes, drained well

2 cups cooked asparagus, cut into 1-inch pieces

1 Tbsp. each Italian seasoning and salt

1 tsp. pepper

$1/2$ cup marsala wine

$1 1/2$ cup chicken stock

Cornstarch wash (equal amounts cornstarch and water)

16 oz. fusilli pasta, cooked and drained

Grated Romano cheese

☞ Over high heat, sauté the mushrooms, green onions, and garlic in the oil until tender. Add the olives and tomatoes. Heat thoroughly. Add asparagus and dry spices, stirring constantly. Add marsala wine to deglaze, then add chicken stock. Add cornstarch wash to thicken to desired consistency. Pour over pasta and mix; sprinkle with cheese, and serve hot.

Serves 6

California Asparagus Commission CALIFORNIA ASPARAGUS SANDWICH

LEMON AIOLI

1/2 tsp. finely chopped lemon zest
1 Tbsp. fresh lemon juice
2 finely chopped cloves garlic
1/8 tsp. salt
1/3 cup mayonnaise
1 Tbsp. olive oil

SANDWICH

8 squares focaccia bread, about 5 x 5-inch split
    (other rolls may be used)
1 1/2 cups baby arugula or lettuce leaves
1 cup julienned roasted red pepper
8 oz. mozzarella cheese, cut into 1/4-inch slices
16 asparagus spears, cooked tender-crisp
4 slices 1/8-inch-thick pancetta or 8 slices thick
    bacon cooked almost crisp and broken into
    2-3-inch pieces

☞ Bring all ingredients to room temperature.

Make aioli, whisking together zest, juice, garlic and salt. Whisk in mayonnaise and oil. Spread smooth side of each focaccia square with a generous $1/2$ tablespoon aioli. Divide remaining ingredients among 4 squares of focaccia, layered in order listed. Top with remaining 4 squares of focaccia. Cut each sandwich in half into two triangles. Sandwiches can be served at room temperature or warmed for a few minutes in a 450°F oven.

Serves 4

45

Bianca Solorzano's
ASPARAGUS SAUTÉ

1 lb. asparagus, cut into ¹/₂-inch diagonal pieces
3 Tbsp. peanut oil
³/₄ cup raw shrimp, peeled and deveined
5 sliced mushrooms
2 tsp. cornstarch
¹/₄ cup chicken or vegetable broth
2 Tbsp. soy sauce
1 Tbsp. sherry
1 dash sugar
Salt and pepper to taste

☞ Heat half of the oil in a wok or skillet and cook asparagus until bright green. Push asparagus to one side.

Add remaining oil and sauté shrimp and mushrooms for 2 minutes. In a small bowl, combine cornstarch, broth, soy sauce, sherry, and sugar. Stir into asparagus mixture.

Season with salt and pepper. Cook 1-2 minutes longer. Serve over rice.

Serves 2-4

46

Rich Ibarra's
"Sloppy 'GRAS"

1 lb. ground beef
1/4 lb. sliced mushrooms
1 10³/4-oz. can cream of mushroom soup
1/2 tsp. basil
3/4 lb. thinly sliced cooked asparagus
4-5 thinly sliced green onions
1/4 cup milk

☞ Brown the ground beef and mushrooms in medium skillet. Drain fat. Add mushroom soup, basil, asparagus, green onions, and milk. Lower temperature to simmer. Cook 6-8 minutes or until heated through.

Serve over toasted hamburger buns, rice, or noodles.

Serves 4

ASPARASTRATA KASSANDRA

1 finely chopped onion

4 cups thinly sliced asparagus, cut diagonally

6 cups 1-inch cubed white bread

2 cups each shredded cheddar cheese and shredded jack cheese

7 eggs

2 1/2 cups milk

2 tsp. each salt and paprika

1/2 tsp. each pepper, garlic powder, and dry mustard

1 tsp. oregano

☞ Mix onion, asparagus, bread, 1 cup cheddar cheese, and 1 cup jack cheese in a bowl (reserve remaining cheese). Set aside.

Combine the eggs, milk, salt, paprika, pepper, garlic powder, dry mustard, and oregano, mixing well. Add to asparagus mixture and mix well.

Pour mixture into 9 x 13-inch dish sprayed with non-stick cooking spray. Top with remaining cheddar and jack cheeses. Bake at 350°F for 1 hour, or until golden brown. Let rest for 10 minutes before serving.

Serves 12 as a brunch or lunch dish,
15 as a side dish.

San Joaquin Valley
ENCHILADAS

2-3 lbs. fresh asparagus, cut into 1-inch pieces

12 tortillas

1/2 cup oil

1/2 cup each butter and flour

3-4 cups chicken broth

1 cup sour cream

1/2 cup green taco sauce

3 cups grated jack cheese

3 cups cooked and shredded chicken

1/2 cup chopped onions

Parmesan cheese

☞ Blanch and drain asparagus; set aside.

Cook each tortilla in a large oiled skillet to soften. Set aside to cool and drain.

In saucepan, melt butter. Blend in flour and add chicken broth. Cook until thick and bubbly, stirring constantly. Add sour cream and taco sauce. Heat thoroughly.

Mix together 2 cups jack cheese, chicken, onion, and asparagus. Divide mixture evenly among tortillas; top each with 3 tablespoons sauce and roll. Place seam-side down in 9 x 13-inch dish. Sprinkle with remaining jack cheese, then cover with a layer of Parmesan cheese and the remaining sauce. Bake at 425°F for 25 minutes.

Serves 6

Asparagus QUICHE LAMPERTHEIMER

BATTER
7 oz. flour
1/2 tsp. salt
3 egg yolks
41/2 oz. clarified butter
4 soup spoons water

FILLING
26 oz. asparagus, cut into bite-sized pieces
14 oz. vegetable stock
41/2 oz. cream fraiche or sour cream
4 eggs
1 bunch finely minced chervil
31/2 oz. grated Emmentaler cheese
Salt and pepper to taste
1-2 pinches nutmeg
4 oz. cherry tomatoes, cut in half
41/2 oz. minced cooked ham
Parsley (optional)

52

☞ Combine batter ingredients and refrigerate for 30 minutes.

Heat oven to 350°F. Cook asparagus in vegetable stock for 5 minutes. Drain well.

Mix cream, eggs, chervil, cheese, salt, pepper, and nutmeg together.

Roll out batter and place in bottom of a quiche pan. Bake for 10-minutes. Remove and fill the form with asparagus, tomatoes, and ham. Top with cream mixture.

Bake for 25-30 minutes. Garnish with parsley.

Serves 4

This recipe was demonstrated by the Chuchi Lampertheimer Spargelrunde (men's cook club of Lampertheim, Germany) at the 2002 Stockton Asparagus Festival. The German word for asparagus is spargel. *They loosely call themselves "the round table of asparagus friends."*

53

Dave Walker and Lois Hart's
ASPARAGUS
PESTO and PASTA

8 oz. fine textured spaghetti
3 Tbsp. olive oil
1 lb. fresh asparagus, steamed
3 fresh basil leaves
$1/4$ cup grated Parmesan cheese
$1/4$ cup chopped pecans
1 small clove garlic
$1/4$ tsp. salt

☞ Cook spaghetti *al dente* and drain. Add 1 tablespoon olive oil to hot drained spaghetti, toss, and transfer to warmed serving dish. Place remaining oil, asparagus, basil, cheese, pecans, garlic, and salt in blender. Blend until smooth. Serve over warm spaghetti.

Serves 4

54

Asparagus Commission
SCALLOPSPARAGUS STIR-FRY

3/4 cup chicken broth
1 Tbsp. cornstarch
1 tsp. soy sauce
3/4 lb. sea scallops cut in half
1 cup sliced button or oyster mushrooms
1 clove garlic finely chopped
1 tsp. sesame oil
3/4 lb. cooked fresh asparagus cut into 2-inch pieces
1 cup cherry tomato halves
2-3 thin green onions sliced diagonally
Pepper to taste
2 cups hot cooked rice

☞ Combine chicken broth, cornstarch, and soy sauce; set aside.

Stir-fry scallops, mushrooms, and garlic in oil about 4 minutes. Stir in cornstarch mixture. Cook, stirring until sauce thickens. Add drained asparagus, tomatoes, green onions, and pepper; heat thoroughly. Serve over rice.

Serves 4

55

ENTRÉES: *Asparagus Front and Center*

Brazilian BLADES OF 'GRAS

4 Tbsp. butter or margarine
1 lb. flank steak, cut into 1-inch cubes
2 medium red onions, chopped
1 tsp. minced garlic
6 cups diced asparagus
2 lbs. fresh mushrooms, sliced
3/4 cup red wine
1 Tbsp. red wine vinegar
8 oz. canned tomato sauce
Salt and pepper to taste
3 cups sour cream

In large skillet melt butter. Add meat, onions, and garlic, and sauté at medium-high heat for 5-6 minutes or until meat is browned. Add asparagus and mushrooms; cook until asparagus is tender but crisp. Add wine, vinegar, tomato sauce, salt, and pepper. Cook until heated through. Just before serving, add the sour cream and heat—do not boil.

Serve over noodles or steamed rice.

Serves 6

ENTRÉES: *Asparagus Front and Center*

Asparagus
RICE CASSEROLE

1 1/2 cups each water and chicken stock

1 tsp. salt

1 lb. asparagus, cut into bite-sized pieces

2 Tbsp. melted butter

1 chopped small onion

3 minced cloves garlic

1 cup uncooked long-grain rice

1/2 cup each diced red bell pepper and grated
   Parmesan cheese

☞ Mix all ingredients together, then pour into 2-quart casserole and cover.

Bake at 400°F for 20 minutes. Stir and bake another 20 minutes.

Serves 4

Asparagus "WOODCHUCK"

> 1 cup shredded Jarlsberg cheese
>
> 3 Tbsp. each lemon juice and flour
>
> 1 1/2 cups ready-to-serve chunky tomato soup
>   (add no water)
>
> 1/2 tsp. dry mustard
>
> 1 4 1/4 oz. can chopped olives
>
> 1 lb. sliced small new potatoes
>
> 1 lb. asparagus
>
> Lemon and olive slices (optional)

☞ Mix cheese with lemon juice and set aside. Mix flour, soup, dry mustard, and olives together. Set aside.

Place potatoes in a large pot with enough water to cover both potatoes and asparagus. Bring to a boil and cook potatoes 4-5 minutes until crisp but tender. Add asparagus and after water has returned to boiling, cook vegetables together 3 minutes. Drain.

58

Meanwhile, combine cheese with olive mixture and warm gently over medium heat, stirring 3-4 minutes or until cheese is just melted. Topping will be thick and rich—serve at once.

Serve vegetables on platter topped with cheese. Garnish with lemon and olive slices. Or, divide vegetables and sauce on warm dinner plates for individual servings.

Serves 4-6

Uptown
ASPARAGUS TACOS

l lb. asparagus, cut into 1-inch pieces

2 Tbsp. diced red bell pepper

1-1^1/$_2$ Tbsp. chili powder or 1 1-oz. envelope taco
  seasoning mix

^{1}/$_2$ cup water

1 15-oz. can reduced sodium black beans,
  rinsed and drained

^{1}/$_2$ cup chopped walnuts

Salt to taste

8 warmed large flour tortillas or 8 crisp taco shells

1 cup grated reduced-fat cheddar cheese

Tomato salsa

Shredded iceberg lettuce

☞ Coat a large nonstick skillet with cooking spray. Over medium-high heat, cook asparagus and pepper for 4-5 minutes, stirring frequently. Stir in spice, water, and beans. Cover the pan and cook 2 minutes. Add the walnuts and stir for about 1 minute more. Add salt.

Divide the filling among the tortillas, using about 1/3 cup filling in each taco. Top the filling with 2 tablespoons grated cheese.

Pass salsa and lettuce at the table to add to the tacos as desired.

Serves 4

Green, Black, and Red PIZZA

> 8 oz. asparagus
> 1 cup shredded Jarlsberg cheese
> 1/2 cup non-fat ricotta cheese
> 1 cup marinara or pizza sauce, seasoned
>   with 1/4-1/2 tsp. garlic powder
> 1 12-inch (10-oz.) prebaked thin pizza crust
> 1 cup sliced olives

☞ Preheat oven to 425°F.

Remove 3-inch tips from asparagus spears and chop remaining asparagus into 1/2-inch pieces. Place all asparagus in boiling water and cook 3 minutes. Drain immediately and plunge in ice water. Drain again and set aside.

Thoroughly mix cheeses. Set aside.

Spread seasoned sauce evenly on crust, leaving $1/2$-inch edge. Arrange asparagus tips like spokes of a wheel. Evenly sprinkle on asparagus and olives. Drop a heaping tablespoon of cheese mixture around the edge of the pizza and in the center. There should be 9-10 cheese mounds.

Bake about 12 minutes.

Serves 4-6

Martin Yan's ASPARAGUS with SWEET SESAME DRESSING

> 1 lb. asparagus, cut into 2-inch diagonal slices
>   and cooked until tender-crisp
>
> DRESSING
> 2 Tbsp. packed light brown sugar
> 1 Tbsp. each sesame oil, soy sauce, rice vinegar,
>   sesame paste, and mirin (Japanese sweet rice wine)
> 1 Tbsp. toasted sesame seeds

☞ Combine dressing ingredients in a small saucepan. Heat over medium heat until sugar and sesame paste are dissolved. Simmer, stirring constantly, until slightly thickened, about 1-2 minutes.

Arrange asparagus on a serving platter. Spoon dressing over asparagus, sprinkle with sesame seeds, and serve immediately.

Serves 4

ROASTED, BBQed, or PAN-FRIED ASPARAGUS

> 2 lbs. asparagus
> Extra virgin olive oil

☞ Toss asparagus spears in olive oil. Place asparagus in a jellyroll pan to bake in a preheated 425°F oven, place on the grill to barbeque, or in a large skillet to pan-fry. Cook until crisp but tender. Check carefully, no style of cooking should take more than 10-15 minutes, or even less.

OPTIONS: Sprinkle with minced garlic, sea salt, coarse pepper, dried thyme, or chopped fresh thyme.

After asparagus is plated, asparagus may be drizzled with balsamic syrup (reduced balsamic vinegar).

Lemon wedges or quartered tomatoes can be used as garnish.

Serves 6-8

Asparagus
LASAGNA

1-2 lbs. fresh or frozen asparagus,
cut into 1-inch pieces
3 Tbsp. butter
2 green onions, chopped
12 oz. fresh mushrooms, chopped
1/4 cup flour
1 tsp. salt
1/4 tsp. cayenne pepper
2 1/2 cups milk
8 oz. lasagna noodles, cooked
2 cups cottage cheese
2 cups shredded jack cheese (or more)
1/2-1 cup grated Parmesan cheese (or more)
Black pepper to taste (optional)

66

☞ Cook asparagus and drain; let cool.

Preheat oven to 325°F.

Melt butter in medium saucepan. Add onions and mushrooms and cook over medium heat, about 5 minutes. Blend in flour, salt, and cayenne pepper. Gradually stir in milk. Cook sauce until thickened for additional 5 minutes.

Spread ½ cup sauce in greased 9 x 13-inch baking dish. Layer noodles (season with pepper for more spicy flavor), asparagus, cottage cheese, jack cheese, a third of the remaining sauce, and Parmesan cheese. Repeat to make three layers.

Bake for 45 minutes. Let stand 20 minutes before cutting to serve.

Serves 12

Asparagus
BRUSCHETTA

1 cup ricotta cheese

2 Tbsp. oil-packed sundried tomatoes, drained and finely chopped

1 Tbsp. each diced black olives and chopped parsley

1 green onion, minced

1/4 tsp. each grated lemon peel and lemon pepper

1 loaf crusty Italian or French bread

1 lb. cooked asparagus, cut into 4-inch pieces

1/2 cup shredded mozzarella cheese

1 Tbsp. each olive oil, balsamic vinegar, and snipped basil leaves

1 clove garlic, pressed

Cherry tomatoes for garnish

☞ Preheat oven to 400°F.

Combine ricotta, sundried tomatoes, olives, parsley, onion, lemon peel, and lemon pepper. Mix well and set aside.

Cut the bread in thirds horizontally. Trim crusts so the bread sits level. Cut each piece in half crosswise to make 6 pieces. Spread the cut sides of the bread with the ricotta mixture, arrange asparagus on top, then sprinkle with mozzarella.

Place on a baking sheet. Bake for 5 minutes.

Combine oil, vinegar, basil, and garlic. Drizzle over the bruschetta. Garnish and serve.

Serves 6

CHICKEN ASPARAGUS BAKE

5 Tbsp. each butter and flour

1 1/2 cups chicken broth

6-oz. can mushrooms, drained

Dash pepper

2 large chicken breasts, cooked and sliced

1 lb. cooked fresh asparagus spears

1/4 cup dry bread crumbs

2 Tbsp. each snipped parsley, toasted slivered almonds, and melted butter

 Preheat oven to 375°F.

Melt butter; blend in flour. Add chicken broth; cook and stir until mixture is thickened. Add mushrooms and pepper.

Place chicken in bottom of 6 x 10 x 1 1/2-inch baking dish. Drizzle with half the mushroom sauce. Arrange asparagus spears over sauce, then pour on remaining sauce.

Combine crumbs, parsley, almonds, and melted butter. Sprinkle over casserole. Bake 20 minutes.

 Serves 4

Entrées: *Asparagus Front and Center*

ROLLED STEAK
Stuffed with Asparagus

2 Tbsp. each horseradish and minced garlic

3-4 lbs. flank steak, butterflied

1 lb. asparagus spears

☞ Spread horseradish and garlic on the steak. Arrange spears in a single row over the spread. Roll tightly and tie.

Roast in 350°F oven for 1 hour. Remove from oven and let stand 10 minutes before slicing.

Serves 6-8

DESSERTS & OTHER GOODIES: You're Kidding! There's Asparagus in Here?

All recipes require cleaned and trimmed asparagus.

Kitty's ASPARAGUS MARGARITA

1 lb. fresh asparagus, blanched and chopped

10 oz. margarita mix

6 oz. tequila

8 oz. crushed ice

1 lime, quartered

1 tsp. seasoned salt

6 spears asparagus, blanched

 Place chopped asparagus, margarita mix, tequila, and crushed ice into blender; blend until smooth.

Rub top rim of 6 glasses with lime. Place salt on plate and dip glasses to cover rims with salt. Garnish with asparagus spear and serve.

Serves 6

GOODIES: *You're Kidding! There's Asparagus in Here?*

No-Guilt ASPARAGUS GUACAMOLE

4 cups fresh or frozen asparagus, cut into
1-inch pieces
1 clove garlic, minced
2 tsp. lime juice
1/4 cup canned, chopped green chilies
1/2 tsp. each salt and cumin
2 Tbsp. finely chopped onion
1/2 cup chopped, seeded tomato

☞ Cook asparagus in small amount of water until tender. Drain well and cool thoroughly.

In food processor or blender, process asparagus, garlic, lime juice, chilies, salt, and cumin until mixture is smooth, about 30 seconds.

Remove mixture from food processor and stir in onion and tomato. Chill thoroughly before serving with tortilla chips, cut vegetables, chicken, or seafood.

Yield: 2 cups
This recipe was shared by The Michigan
Asparagus Advisory Board

GOODIES: *You're Kidding! There's Asparagus in Here?*

Low-Fat ASPARAGUS MUFFINS

1 cup flour
1 Tbsp. baking powder
1 tsp. cinnamon
1/4 tsp. salt
3/4 cup Grape Nut cereal
1/4 cup rolled oats
1 cup fat-free milk
1 egg, slightly beaten
1/2 cup very chunky applesauce
1 cup chopped asparagus
1/2 cup shredded carrots
1/2 cup sugar
2 Tbsp. melted margarine
1/2 cup dried cranberries or raisins (optional)

👉 Heat oven to 400°F.

Mix flour, baking powder, cinnamon, and salt in large bowl. Mix in cereal, oats, and milk. Stir in egg, applesauce, asparagus, carrots, sugar, and margarine. Fill muffin cups to two-thirds full.

Bake 20 minutes, or until golden brown.

Yield: Approximately 12 muffins

GOODIES: *You're Kidding! There's Asparagus in Here?*

Aspara-Chocolate Chip
SURPRISE COOKIES

2³/4 cups flour

1 tsp. each salt and baking soda

³/4 cup each packed brown sugar and sugar

1 cup butter, softened

3 eggs

2 tsp. vanilla

2 cups grated asparagus

1 cup chopped nuts

2 cups chocolate chips

☞ Mix together flour, salt, and baking soda. Set aside.

Cream the sugars with the butter for several minutes. Add the eggs and vanilla, beat well. Add the flour mixture, beat well. Fold in the asparagus, nuts, and chocolate chips.

Drop by rounded tablespoon onto greased cookie sheet.

Bake at 375°F. for 12-15 minutes, or until golden brown.

Yield: Approximately 4¹/2 dozen cookies

GOODIES: *You're Kidding! There's Asparagus in Here?*

ASPARAGUS SALSA

1 red bell pepper, minced
1 green bell pepper, minced
1 13-oz. can pre-sliced, peeled tomatoes
4 Roma tomatoes, minced
1 Tbsp. Tabasco sauce
Salt to taste
Chopped green onions to taste
1 cup minced fresh asparagus

☞ In a bowl, mix all ingredients well. Refrigerate at least 1 hour, then season to taste. Serve with chips.

Yield: Approximately 5-6 cups

GOODIES: *You're Kidding! There's Asparagus in Here?*

Narsai David's ASPARAGUS ICE BOX PICKLES

Copyright © 2002 by Narsai M. David

---

1 1/2 lbs. asparagus spears
1/4 tsp. red pepper flakes
1 Tbsp. pickling spice
3-4 garlic cloves, bruised
1 cup white wine vinegar
3/4 cup water
2 Tbsp. sugar

☞ Cut asparagus to fit in a wide-mouth 1-quart canning jar. Fill jar with asparagus, tips up. Place red pepper flakes, pickling spice, and garlic cloves in the jar.

Heat vinegar, water, and sugar only until boiling. Pour hot liquid into the jar. Set aside to cool; refrigerate.

NOTE: This is an icebox pickle that has not been sterilized. It must remain refrigerated until consumed.

Yield: 1 quart

GOODIES: *You're Kidding! There's Asparagus in Here?*

Pickled
ASPARAGUS

8 lbs. asparagus spears, trimmed to fit 8 pint jars

8 cloves garlic

1 quart each vinegar and water

4 Tbsp. salt

1 Tbsp. whole, mixed pickling spice

☞ Blanch asparagus spears 1 minute. Cool in ice water.

Pack clean, hot pint jars with 1 clove garlic and asparagus.

Heat vinegar, water, salt, and spice to simmering, then pour over asparagus. Leave 1/2 inch headspace. Wipe rim of jar with clean cloth.

GOODIES: *You're Kidding! There's Asparagus in Here?*

Process in a water bath for 15 minutes at 170°F. (See page 94.)

OPTIONS: Add fresh or dried dillweed along with garlic. If dill is used, pickling spice is optional. Or, add 6 black peppercorns, 1 dried red chili pepper, and 1 teaspoon dried dill seed or fresh dill to each jar.

Yield: 8 pints

81

GOODIES: *You're Kidding! There's Asparagus in Here?*

Asparagus
CORN RELISH

1 cup chopped asparagus

2 cups corn kernels

1/2 cup each chopped onion and chopped celery

1 cup chopped red and/or green peppers

1 Tbsp. mustard seed

1 tsp. each celery seed and turmeric

1 cup vinegar

1/2 cup water

☞ Combine all ingredients. Cook until vegetables are tender.

Store in refrigerator for up to one week.

Yield: Approximately 6 cups

82

Kassy's
ASPARAGUS SALSA

Chop and mix together:
1 medium red pepper
1 medium green pepper
3 golden pepperoncini
3 cooked asparagus spears
2 red tomatoes

ADD:
Juice of 1 lime
Salt and pepper to taste

 Mix together and chill well. Serve with chips.

Yield: Approximately 2 cups

GOODIES: *You're Kidding! There's Asparagus in Here?*

Asparagus
BEAN RELISH

1 10-oz. can each garbanzo beans and kidney beans,
   drained and rinsed

9 asparagus spears, cut into 1 1/2-inch pieces,
   blanched and cooled

1 small yellow onion, diced

2-3 Tbsp. extra virgin olive oil

2 Tbsp. red wine vinegar

Salt and pepper to taste

☞ Combine all ingredients and mix well.

Refrigerate.

Yield: Approximately 5 cups

GOODIES: *You're Kidding! There's Asparagus in Here?*

Bread and Butter
ASPARAGUS PICKLES

¹/3 cup salt

3 cups distilled vinegar

2 cups sugar

2 Tbsp. mustard seed

2 tsp. each turmeric and celery seed

1 tsp. each ground ginger and peppercorns

5 lbs. asparagus, cut into 1-inch pieces

10 small onions, thinly sliced

☞ Bring salt, vinegar, sugar, mustard, turmeric, and celery seeds to boil with ginger and peppercorns. Add asparagus and onions and bring to another boil. Pack hot into hot jars, leaving ¹/4-inch headspace. Remove air bubbles. Process 15 minutes in boiling water bath. (See page 94.)

Yield: 4-5 pints

GOODIES: *You're Kidding! There's Asparagus in Here?*

Asparagus-Banana
CHUTNEY

1 cup chopped asparagus

4 bananas, sliced

1 red pepper, chopped

1 green pepper, chopped

1 medium onion, chopped

2 Jalapeño peppers, chopped

1 1/2 cups vinegar

1 tsp. each celery seed and chopped garlic

1 Tbsp. mustard seed

☞ Combine all ingredients and cook until thick.

Store in refrigerator for up to one week.

Yield: approximately 6 cups

GOODIES: *You're Kidding! There's Asparagus in Here?*

Asparagus
WINE CAKE

1 18.5 oz. pkg. yellow cake mix

3 eggs

1 tsp. nutmeg

1 3/4 oz. pkg. vanilla instant pudding

3/4 cup each vegetable oil and cream sherry

1/4 cup asparagus purée

1/2 cup finely chopped asparagus

☞ Combine all ingredients, except for the finely chopped asparagus, and mix with electric beater for 5 minutes at medium speed. Fold in finely chopped asparagus. Pour batter into greased tube pan.

Bake at 350°F for 45 minutes, or until done. Cool in pan 5 minutes before turning on to rack. Cool; sprinkle with powdered sugar.

Yield: 12-16 slices

87

GOODIES: *You're Kidding! There's Asparagus in Here?*

Asparagus
POPPY SEED LOAF

STREUSEL TOPPING
1/4 cup each sugar and lightly packed brown sugar
1 Tbsp. flour
2 Tbsp. butter, room temperature

LOAF
2 cups flour
1/2 tsp. each salt and baking soda
3/4 tsp. baking powder
1/4 cup butter, room temperature
2 eggs, room temperature
3/4 cup sugar
1 cup sour cream
1 1/2 tsp. vanilla extract
1/4 cup each cream sherry and poppy seeds
3/4 cup finely chopped fresh asparagus

GOODIES: *You're Kidding! There's Asparagus in Here?*

☞ Preheat oven to 375°F.

Combine all streusel topping ingredients and mix until crumbly. Set aside.

Sift together flour, salt, baking soda, and baking powder. Set aside.

In a large mixing bowl, beat the butter, eggs, and sugar until well blended. Mix in sour cream, vanilla, cream sherry, and poppy seeds until well mixed. Fold in sifted ingredients and asparagus. Pour batter into a 5 x 9-inch loaf pan that has been lightly buttered and floured. Sprinkle evenly with streusel topping mixture.

Bake for 55-60 minutes, or until a toothpick inserted into center comes out clean.

Yield: 1 loaf

89

GOODIES: *You're Kidding! There's Asparagus in Here?*

Asparagus
SHERRY CAKE

3 cups sifted flour

2 tsp. cinnamon

1 1/4 tsp. salt

1 tsp. baking powder

1 1/2 tsp. baking soda

1 cup oil

2 cups sugar

3 eggs

1 tsp. each vanilla and lemon peel

4 Tbsp. cooking sherry

2 cups finely diced asparagus

1 1/2 cups chopped pecans

1 cup chopped fresh cranberries

1/4 cup powdered sugar

1 Tbsp. milk

90

☞ Preheat oven to 325°F.

Combine flour, cinnamon, salt, baking powder, and baking soda. Mix well; set aside.

Beat together oil, sugar, and eggs. Add vanilla, lemon peel, sherry, and asparagus. Fold in dry ingredients; mix well. Add pecans and cranberries.

Pour batter into 10-inch greased and floured tube pan.

Bake for 1 hour and 15 minutes. Cool before removing from pan.

Combine powdered sugar with milk to make frosting. Place cake on cake plate and decorate with frosting.

Serves 12

GOODIES: *You're Kidding! There's Asparagus in Here?*

ASPARABREAD

3 cups flour
1 tsp. each salt and baking soda
1/4 tsp. baking powder
1 cup oil
3 eggs
2 cups each sugar and grated asparagus
2 tsp. vanilla
1/2 tsp. each nutmeg and allspice
3 tsp. cinnamon
1/2 cup chopped nuts

☞ Preheat oven to 350°F.

Sift together flour, salt, baking soda, and baking powder. Set aside. Beat together oil, eggs, sugar, asparagus, and vanilla: add to dry ingredients. Add spices and nuts; mix by hand until ingredients are moistened. Divide batter into 2 greased 5 x 9-inch loaf pans.

Bake for 1 hour or until toothpick inserted in center of loaf comes out clean.

VARIATION: Substitute 1 cup crushed drained pineapple for 1 cup grated asparagus.

Yield: 2 loaves

GOODIES: *You're Kidding! There's Asparagus in Here?*

ASPARA-SQUARES

2 cups flour
1 tsp. each baking soda and cinnamon
1/2 tsp. each salt, cloves and nutmeg
2 cups packed brown sugar
1/2 cup margarine, softened
1 3/4 cups cooked, diced asparagus
2 egg whites
1 cup chopped dried apricots
1/2 cup chopped walnuts

☞ Combine flour, baking soda, cinnamon, salt, cloves and nutmeg. Set aside.

In a large bowl cream together sugar and margarine. Add asparagus and egg whites. Add flour mixture. Mix well. Add apricots and walnuts. Mix well.

Pour mixture into a 9 x 13-inch baking dish coated with cooking spray. Bake at 350°F for 35 minutes, or until done.

Cut into squares and sprinkle with powdered sugar.

Yield: 12-15 servings

GOODIES: *You're Kidding! There's Asparagus in Here?*

☞ Water Bath Process

1. Prepare lids according to manufacturer's instructions.

2. Fill clean hot jars with asparagus to within 1/2 inch of the rim.

3. Cover the asparagus with hot liquid or brine. Leave 1/2 inch headspace (the distance between the contents and the rim of the jar.)

4. Remove air bubbles by running a plastic knife or spatula between the asparagus and the jar.

5. Clean rim and threads of the jar.

6. Place heated lid on jar and secure with a hot ring band. Screw the band down so that it is hand tight.

the Asparagus Festival Cookbook

7. Place jars in a water bath or deep kettle with a rack. The water bath should be about half full before loading. Water should be very hot but not boiling. Add enough water to cover the tops of the jars by at least 1 inch.

8. Begin to time when the water bath temperature reaches 180°F.

9. As you take the jar from the water bath, hold level, but do not disturb the seal. Leave the ring bands on the jars until thoroughly cooled.

10. Place the hot jars, well separated, on a rack or folded towel away from drafts or cool surfaces. Remove rings to store jars.

95

☞ Conversion Chart

LIQUID
1 tablespoon = 15 ml
1/2 cup = 4 fl ounces = 125 ml
1 cup = 8 fl ounces = 250 ml

DRY
1/4 cup = 4 tablespoons = 2 ounces = 60 g
1 cup = 1/2 pound = 8 ounces = 250 g

FLOUR
1/2 cup = 60 g
1 cup = 4 ounces = 125 g

TEMPERATURE
400°F = 200°C = gas mark 6
375°F = 190°C = gas mark 5
350°F = 175°C = gas mark 4

MISCELLANEOUS
2 tablespoons butter = 1 oz = 30 g
1 inch = 2.5 cm
all-purpose flour = plain flour
baking soda = bicarbonate of soda
heavy cream = double cream
sugar = caster sugar

Printed in the United States
by Baker & Taylor Publisher Services